When

I Thought It

Was

Myles Hall

"Published by in the United States By Myles Publishing Company 2022"

Copyright © 2022 Myles Hall

ISBN: 979-8-9857916-0-0

Tribute

In loving memory of my brother,

Isaiah Earl Hall

(1995 - 2021)

Preface

*T*his book has been a beautiful journey from beginning to end. Happiness resides in me knowing this is the first piece of art I offer this world. Stepping out of my bubble and into reality represents my story, and what Broken Hearts Heal stands for.

Before anything else, let me start off with an introduction. My name is Myles Hall. I am 21 years young born and raised in Vallejo, CA. I lived in Vallejo for my formative years and moved to Fairfield, CA in my teenage years. I am a brand owner, writer, creative, video game enthusiast, and much more. My main purpose on this earth is to help and inspire people at their lowest as I should have done for myself.

The reason I created Broken Hearts Heal and When I Thought It Was was to provide an outlet for people to re-jumpstart their life again. My goal is for my brand to become the ignition for everyone beginning their journey in life.

Suppose you can only take one thing from this book: Broken Hearts Heal. I know this sounds cliche coming from a brand owner but hear me out. Everyone has a scar from somewhere from somebody. The only way to recover and find fulfilment in life is to build that mental fortitude to understand not your scars, but how you heal define who you are, hence Broken Hearts Heal.

In When I Thought It Was, I give you 77 poems that illustrate my story and the story of others who are unsure of self when entering adulthood. *The writing process took an excruciating 25 month process of failure, revision, and more failure from March 2021 to April 2023. Topics that are discussed include: depression, drugs, loneliness, reflection, and more. To be honest, this book isn't for everyone. It can be alot to digest and handle in certain moments. I recommend all readers to take your time and read at your own pace.*

I hope all readers enjoy this piece of writing and take something away from it. Thank you for supporting me in this capacity. I have the utmost love and respect toward anyone giving their time to let my passions come to life. If you wish to support me any further, go to brokenheartsheal.com and buy a hoodie, teddy bear, or learn more about my brand. Follow my socials and get the word around of who I am and what I will accomplish.

Furthermore, I present When I Thought It Was, Written by Myles Hall.

Socials:

Instagram - Myleslee_02

Twitter - Myleslee_02

Tick-Tok - Myleslee-02

Table of Contents

Chapter 1

Beginning of the End

Funeral

Need love

Where can I find it

What happened to me

No time to solve it

My daughter's warmth

My momma smile

All went away

Way too fast

Solace when I close my eyes

Everyone is subject to lies

Led the life that was wanted

Can't walk on my soil

Altered dreams

Where I was displaced from me

Honestly

Not the person I was meant to be

Kills the intuition to finally see

Say your goodbye

See me for me

Myles Hall

Almost had

What everyone wanted in me

I

Over the mountains

Saw it all

Peace was just a cause

Walking down my street

Wondering who was gone

Starred at the ground

Concrete held my frown

Closed my eyes

For the final time

Pixie dust held me close

For the last time

Wish it felt surreal

Sky won't know what's forreal

Convo with G

Can't talk to you
That sun isn't clear
Only opened wide
When you were here

If I hug myself
You wouldn't change
This pressure could crush
Any dream in place
Cutting down these bushes
Day by day
Wanting to see that picture
Only you can make

My scent in these people mind
Remembered like you and I
When the patch grew
Couldn't count on you

Gathered this pain
Made pride out of it

When I Thought It Was

Why thank you

I'm the reason

I'm here

Speak clearly

Won't remember your stare

Just promise me

I'll make it out for them

Now you're gone

Continue hunting

For that heart

You said was coming

Godspeed

Life at Godspeed

The barrier cracked

I was at ease

Disturbed upon my first life

Introduced into this fight

When seasons change

Hid feelings of being away

Presence stood tall every day

Head against the casket

Cried when I heard what happened

People were chained

Past can't be erased

Godspeed to anyone

Who hasn't stayed sane

Never

Never walked that path

Jittery my heart can't stand

Shaking every day

Hope my high won't land

Once midnight

My brain can finally rest

Cover on me trying to protect myself

Process is long

Pray every night

Deep down

I lost the fight

Gave all I had

With my weight up high

Shattered down

Wish it was our time

Feeling(The 6th Sense)

Best way to feel

Is not to think at all

Numbness on this plane

Darkness doesn't have weight

Sadness is a genuine place

That delight couldn't save

What was pushed on my plate

Into my mind

These barriers won't break

Somebody saw

When I poured into this rain

This day I was relaxed

In zones the galaxy left attached

Putting my life at ease

Take a glance and see

While my life on hold

Can't end it with passengers in my seat

Let my mind drift off

Autopilot through this life

It told me to land

Why make a trip

If I don't make it back

Damsel in distress

In a world that broke my back

Soaked full of words

From my tongue to my heart

My wants and needs

Something I'll never reach

My head stays low

When they produce another me

In My Head

Swiping through unforeseen lives

Trying to find my match

My lighter couldn't help

She still ran

My soul detached from me

Thoughts in a hearst

For the world to see

They all turned to me

Still in my head

Remembered every word

Don't worry

She won't tell the world

Inhaled too much

Won't cough up what I had

If my time is today

Forever live in my head

No words

I'm single

Wasn't worth the trouble

In and outta lust

My love was muffled

Ran in with another

Let myself win

The game finally over

My scars haunt others

Feelings won't vanish

Steady in a panic

Poured my heart

Life of an addict

Footsteps on top of my grave

Made that difference

Why my heart ain't different

Don't come at me distant

Don't need to wait

Wish I can heal

Beginning of the End

All my fallen brothers

Died before we became fathers

No words

Hope I become my father

Why

Why I fail in my sleep
Why I'm silenced before I speak
Paint pictures of something bleak
Something so strong
Broke my peace
Underlying pressure
Caused us to meet

Shackles on my mind
Instead of my feet
Thought time healed all
Became what nobody wanted in me

Reused lines
Didn't know how to get mines
Made my stance clear
Enough for the world to stare
It wasn't fair

Break up
Roll up

Beginning of the End

Provided a spark

Most at love

When I was far away

Made it so high

The naked eye

Watching my demise

Detractors kept their head high

One day I'll ask why

Kept my hope to survive

Weak

Numbness from head to toe

Is it okay to bleed

Helpless in my weakest state

Alone

These sticks and stones

End up breaking my soul

All this energy

If only I can give

One moment for everything to break

Tides turned

Left me forever blank

Hopeless

Something that was maybe

Becomes someone that never was

Came into this life with everything

Walking out by myself

Deep Thoughts

Final days above us

Exhale

Breath

You better than me

You in your head

Trying to get ahead

Cancel those thoughts

Acting like you ain't win

Above all else

Locked within myself

Need to let go

Chapter 2

Submerged in Hate

Underground

Room full of darkness
A place to grieve in
Casket of pride
Tortured souls close in

Here I am
Between two mediums
With or without sanity
Juggled in the eyes of many
With every step I don't take
Another man will

On another man's will
It said
Fight and die on a hill
See my offering become real

Old Soul

Past life against me

Twitch of a perfect life

Cured the nameless

Was off everything

Me versus the world

Disguised pain in lust

Old soul with nothing left

Cried with a piece of mind

They got a piece of mine

Greed

Garnered everything

Respect

Fame

Rip it apart

Let the world see

Kept the hungry in awe

In the palm of my hand

Possessions all I have

Y'all couldn't see

Saw what you brothers preached

The land of opportunity

Took that chance

Killed by pressure

Just needed your hand

Relinquish yourself for me

A second dream

Do it all again

Won't be able to see

Tear

Tear in my heart

Stroke in my pride

Thorn rippled down from seasons

Understood my treason

Pixie dust in the eyes

Between trenches we fell

Hustlin backwards

Survived for an end

Gave it my all

My horseshoe bent

Could've been lucky

Rather been dead

Years later

All the same

Granite turned lead

Sorry in advance

Lied if they fire

Remembered for more

If I tried harder

Tear in my heart
Auction off my soul

Final Days/Flowers

5 minutes till sundown

Where my flowers

Paid my dues

Want what's mine

Immortality or death

Decide when I'm there

Last time falling short

Hope wings heal

Cried without em

Too high to notice

Like everybody else

It's too late

Blessings from God

Voided without pape

10 days before November

Thought autumn last forever

My rose knew better

Hustle

Gotta give it up

They want it more than me

Gave it my all

Watch who you bring

Shadows are heartless

Like me

Dipped toes in coal

Holiday spirit turned cold

You have life

Just take mines

Every stone unturned

Clear your mind of what was

Hit my ceiling before the league

My body asleep

Life is now complete

Cared what others said

Become what I won't be

No More to Give

No more to give

My girl heels

Make my heart heal

Became a trick

Pimped out for love

Came back enraged

Hear me out

Fought to know

Stairs don't float

Step by step

Asked for mo

Devil knew a way out

Competition

Stuck in limbo

Know so many

Who hasn't felt pain

Soul beneath the barrier

Shackles over my lower

Thank God

The mission will finally be over

Seemed planned out

Couldn't write

Years on end

Stuck in hell

Help me repent

Love held me in

Figured who escaped

Regret

Palm of my hand

Open for public

Formed a fist

Fought for my life

Against the enraged

Looked as a threat

Released from the cage

Bullet gazed my head

Could I regret

Followed my wishes

Did what I couldn't

God will see

Wanted What I Saw

Saw what I want

Took what I preached

Life at a height

Never before seen

Fitted to a tee

What I need

Don't stop begging

Till I can't breathe

Never was full

Makes me a fool

Revenge is the sweetest joy

Until you black and blue

Lost in life

I need a hand

Release yourself

Took what nobody has

Interlude

Never begun

Why make it last

Wake up tomorrow

No feeling again

Took this chance

Cement these thoughts

Lost between walls

Lead myself out

Woke up to what was

Opened my wounds

Cried softly

Took the fan out my room

Chapter 3

Waiting to Cry Softly

Broke My Face

Please

Break my face

So feelings stay safe

Guard them

Promise me

They won't fly away

Locked in

Didn't take a knee

Finally made it

Disappear with me

Today I'm here

Tomorrow a saint

Newborn in an opposite plane

Heartless

Vivid lies become obscene

Gold when her eyes sang to me

So sudden

Her heart lies within

Just sing to me

Only me

Took what I lost

Gained nothing back

Fought for vengeance

Was all a plan

Roped together in one man's hand

Lost all control

In the field

Never felt that pole

Caught a rose

Fell apart

I'm at fault

Supposed to know

When I Thought It Was

Put agony to rest

Knew best

War-torn memories

Bled my ears

Please God

Get me away from here

Upon the Stars

Enough is enough

Walked them stairs

This galaxy is endless

Stars guided me home

Went to sleep

Array brung me awake

Among the sanctions

Lost footing in space

Eternal

Never let my son

Break

Sleep

Fought through internalized weight

Tomorrow the same way

Can't open my eyes

Without seeing my fate

This pillow saw scars

Not even I can say

Floating in outer planes

Dreams died this way

A way to darkness

Body eagerly awaits

This passage can talk

My dream state can walk

Felt where paradise resides

Found what was lost

Remember this feeling

Knocking up high

Did their job

Late to my cause

Reality or upon stars

Birds fly forever

Room

Stuck on the side

Never could see

Peaked a little

Then left my seed

Pain

Manufactured for the world to see

Forever look up to you

Sickness runs through veins

Jumped from ships

We never escaped

Sorrows within lies

Can't get her back

Paralyzed from the mind

Hurt won't be taken down

Art shadows the unspoken crowd

Stuck in a room

I can't breathe

When I Thought It Was

Thought it was worse

When I couldn't sleep

Locked in my room

Insomnia awaits till god sees

Levels

Encompassed with my dreams
Hold me close and sing
Deciphering through options
Stayed afloat for you

Staircase to heaven
Limit to the sky
Suicidal floors
I won't try

Escaped through hills
Levels to this pain
In this suite
Fighting for what

Was timid to feel
Felt outta place
When angels came to heal

Understood my peak
No way up this ladder

When I Thought It Was

Machine for the wealthy

My oil leaks plenty

This time won't be an issue

Kept my light bright

Mood switched

Draped in insecurity

Lovers knew my peace

Ran out on me

Message won't go obsolete

Writing this poem a whole week

Limelight wasn't to speak

Levels can't protect

The devil's reach

Lonely/Duality

Saw green from far

Behind the closet

Beneath the curb

Outsmart the work

Printed my life on a shirt

Imagined life in stars

Cut marks became scars

Vacuum sealed my heart

Locked within lies

Fertilized the mind

Intertwined with mine

Know my wants

Curate their why

Was a Second Ago

Need you more than myself

Used a blanket

Covered up what was

Unfazed you brought it up

Love started with us

Your heartbeat broke my trust

Said I'm delusional

Knew my truth

Make it last

Let it run away

Nothingness

Never put your heart
In the rearview mirror

Felt lighter
When my pen wrote itself
When pain wrote itself

My seed planted trees
Won't be able to see
Jewel under armor
Anchor beneath seas
Diamond in a ruff
Hope they find me

Withered away my soul
Wasn't the man for most

Outta my mind
Opened the seal
Open your ears
Life cuts deep

Bled to heal

Think too much

Beyond the clouds

Memories could breed light

Don't I seem alright

Well I'm not

Nothing for us

Addiction warmed our heart

Never put my heart

In the rearview mirror

What would happen

If I saw clearer

Disgrace

Walked with a limp
Pimped myself out
The only way

Bullet to my soul
To each it's own
We battle today
Disembowel our own

Between the spectrum of love and hate
Danced with her
She knew my name
Too many thought
They knew my fate
Felt disgraced

Chapter 4

Recollections of Sadness & Pain

Drugs

What I cherish
What I demand
Everything I've longed for
Re-up to feel sore
Heart is empty
Don't make it see-through

Made it out my mind
Walk that vary line
Didn't have enough
Empty at night
Bag still tucked
In my dream
It was enough

Ran through planets and stars
Knew the future is ours
In another atmosphere

It's gonna go away
This trip had a delay

When I Thought It Was

Just give in

Let the game be played

Don't look at me

Any kind of way

Survived in a world

Marginalized since birth

Capitalism took my life

Included was my soul

Tomorrow isn't promised

Death rolled over

Don't let me live

Please let me live

Toxic

Gave me up

I'm not enough

Thought you were the mission

Then why I ran off

Loyalty and respect

Why bother

Played a part you couldn't handle

Had your heart dangling

I'll be glad too

Fetch another one

Why not have two

Animosity tied like a ribbon

We couldn't forget it

Don't worry

Yeah I did

Loose lips can't walk forward

Use my dust for support

Stuck

This cup has me

Never a can be

Learnt to stick and move

Paralyzed victim of what was

Ran the score feeling numb

Antibodies weren't helping nun

Kept my body off the field

Thought this life wasn't real

Mind racing over the hill

Stepping Givenchy

My money ran away

Saw that K in the bank

Delighted to speak

Can't walk your way

Lows can't pick me up

Cup knows me best

Love this pint before death

Double cup to feel safe

Why not make a play

Oh wait

Soldier to the cause

Went up in a blaze

When people move up

Took that joy away

Drifting From Reality

Drifting from reality

Tomorrow made a better me

Need a bad one to fill my plate

My spare is a waste

Chains shackled to my lungs

Smoke to break away

Move outta pain

Who I had

What I need

Took her smile

No bend in her knees

There's no her in me

That perc was tuff

Sorry I had enough

Tried to escape the high

Don't try

Cautious of my steps

Weary of my actions

Deluded in wealth

Trapped with others

Between you and me

Our dreams can walk alone

Let them be

Watch them grow

Played the part

Now you can heal

Man of your dreams

Mom couldn't get enough from me

Doubt/Seconds From Happiness

One...

Two...

Three...

Why they come for me

Come to me

No one to save

Here then I'm out

In the mix whenever it's clout

Saved through negligence

Nurtured my ruin

Never too easy

Never that fluid

Had to blow it

Never easy to forgive

Took his wings

It's grey out there

Stayed since he can't heal

Brittle to nothing

Cloud her judgment

Had us rushing

Took a step back

Hard to see

God couldn't find the man in me

He'll see my way

Pinky Promise

Blinked twice

Now your ahead

Blew me in the wind

Slept without a frame

Snapshot of what came

Broken promises

Who stayed

Stood still when it poured

Showered praises from above

You did what I couldn't

Broke your half

Walked two separate paths

Died for you to live

Your smile isn't enough

Drugs 2

Ran with the tab

Told you

Drugs separate boys from men

Abused so much

Why end it here

The main causality

Left cause of fear

Leave my love

Heal my dove

You delivered enough

Addiction

Addicted to this pain

Tribute to the hope I've slain

Leader of sorrows

An addict

Wondered what was harder

Given up on causes

Can't solve them

Hearts do heal

Mines doesn't have a will

Tell myself every morning

Don't die on this hill

Promise between you and me

You'll do the right thing

Life faded to black

Tugged on my string

Heart of gold

Better than me

Seal your fate with ease

Never fell

You knew why

High Off You

Did what wasn't

I had you

Sipped to the melody

You were brand new

Need you

Us

More than trust

On top of the world

In front of feels

Wheel broken

Don't care to steer

Showed me the ropes

Gave me a reason to stay

Talk to me

Let me see

What others saw

Count my blessings

Ruined you

Ruined me

Toxic 2

You merged off the exit

Without me

Disabled your core

Piece by piece

Attach it back yourself

Demons seeping through skin

An unsudden fate

Locked in that cage

Against these heartless

Which multiples every day

If you love me

You'll move away

Indecisiveness will grant

Your final stray

Pain

Pain on my side

Know it ain't hate

Rib for rib

I'll outlast this pain

They can wait

Wanna be safe

Rather stay dangerous

Weight off my shoulders

They come this way

Can't offer second chances

They ran away

Eternity whispered

Hurt remains awake

Paradise awaits

Forever fall in place

My fate

Set in stone

Hero

Fought for himself

Not a perfect tomorrow

Meet that special someone

Hid their sorrows

Fueling others to bleed

Neglectful to my followers

Message for all

My ceiling rots

Create your own

Be a better you

Please love yourself

More than I love you

Perfect Timing

Pictured the end
Gave it all away
Another spirit took place
Wait
Imagined my life
Frame stood still
Tilted
Ends broke away

Don't have a feeling
Or a heart
I'm the reason
Why give in

Up against the rope
Lemme spark
Up in the sky
Stood my ground

End of my life
You were in it
Timing was perfect
Us had an ending

Wish

Saw that smile

My eyes watered

Been at odds with myself

Rose petals still spin

Life finally moving

Free to roam

Caged bird in the premise

People hate to reason

You were my ignition

My key

Hate it when others can't see

Decided to bail

Need another lock

Took the chance

Often missed

Angel in the sky

Those good times

When I Thought It Was

Alone

Sowing my heart

Back together

Knew long ago

Life wasn't better

In another life

We'll share equal plains

Trade everything to ghost

Know it ain't me

Sorry it took a while

Goodbye, For Now

Care when you cry

Enemies beaten up from inside

All about you

Manifest pain in two

Still there

From similar cloth

Couldn't fake

Threw flowers at you

Pray every day

It broke

Me

Release yourself

Below heavens

Told you I was right

Believe me

Maybe I was wrong

I tried

When I Thought It Was

Lost myself
Second by second
Thought you needed me
When I needed you
My flesh still hurts

Canopy to this world
Through broken glass
Cut so deep
Know it'll last

Why I let her leave
What she meant to me
Everything was closed

Rich but hopeless
Sad I owned it
You were right
Lost you in myself

Left with no remorse
You see it now
Turnaround

Without a frown

Paved the place

You call your own

Won't find another me

Find a better me

Forget about us

Amongst dirt

We thrive

I'ma get us out

On my last day here

No wait

I'm not sane

Told the therapist

The other day

Only you can heal

What you made

Souls locked forever

Tell your father

Mother

When I Thought It Was

Brother

Next lover

We'll be together in the end

Need it more than you

Money

Fame

Success

Leave it all behind

To see your smile

One more time

Take your time

You'll read this one day

Hope you see what I became

My rose will grow inside you again

Until then

Goodbye

For now

When I Thought It Was Explained

When I thought it was
It wasn't

Shined the brightest
Name held no stains
Someone else mistake
It wasn't

Realized my struggle
Skies could read
Life was for me
It wasn't

Dreamed a perfect life
Was a perfect lie
Fallen scars became angels
It wasn't

When I could be me
It wasn't true enough
For the world to see

Chapter 5

Looking for the Other Way Out

Patience

Waited

For scars to heal

Bound to feel

Attack or attach my fears

My world finally still

Preach about sadness

Follow me here

Say it ain't so

Became what never was

Hexagon of hate

Emptied my tank

Beautiful times

My will can tuck me under

Think before I speak

Transversed in solidarity

Inch away from reality

Patience

Trips

Trips to another land
Acid made a better man
Voices laid my head
Wings forced to last

Succumbed to fate
Clouds rejuvenate
Here to stay
Angels made a play

Made it out
On two feet
Pool of tears
I'll shed deep
All for you again

Green Light

Went to the moon

Shell cracked

Atmosphere wasn't blue

Codeine in the liver

Drove the pain away

Dreams mean more

Promise to make it right

Keep you tight

Fought for freedom

We were just alike

Fright trickled off hands

Blessed to see their lends

Once that light turn green

Cd's

Note kept me straight

Took me away

From dying days

Where paradise awaits

Adam to my eve

Sun won't set

Don't leave

Taught me how to plead

Released from future greed

A body lost to the cause

Found under rubber

Unlike my brother

Restraining myself from greatness

I'll get to far

Glass half full

Made amends for people

Who aren't full

Anxiety

Never had a break
Sprung from a neglected soul
Hatched then made a way

When my brother died
Broke me down
Full court press until I rest
My head won't let my heart
Go

Sorry
Too scared to land
Never could stand
Internalized my struggle
Every moment I panic
Soaking up hustle

Pushed against my aging soul
Mind open to the world
Dissect me to my inner core
Won't give in

When I Thought It Was

It's too late

Kept digging for more

When failure looms

Tried to adjust

Calmed my nerves

Take a chance

All for a dream

That doesn't have legs

If you cripple me

Cripple us all

Knew when we met

Could never shake you off

One day

Balance will be restored

Our fight will forever be told

Broke My Face 2

Thought hearts could heal
Then I faced my own
Drive alone
On the 101
Hoping my hands don't go

Destiny set in stone
Operation was cold
Kissed the valley of death
Came back whole

I won
You look at me
Don't look at us
When you finna adjust
With a broken face
Can battle day by day
Saw the finish line
Found a reason to stay

Shy

Spoke to disbelief
Strayed away from those
Who weren't me
Wanted to set the peace

Goner when I stood
Crippled before my chance
Hopeless long ago
Protected from my own
Ego before it grown

Treasured in the eyes of many
Led to believe
Last one to see
Birthed with everything
A child could need
Foreclosed my own
Didn't like how pressure spoke

Know who I am
Don't need to read
Wrote my life
Before I was the lead

Past Self

Fought my adolescence
Just to win
Two jabs to the heart
Blood escaped with wind

Opened my eyes
Felt worthy in self
Nights turned cold
No more give in my throat

On this plane
We leveled out
Jugged and ran me out
Wonder when life took my crown
Line leader who lost his ground

On my soul
It runs deep
Washed tears beyond me
Hid my fade
Facade of the unknown embraced

When I Thought It Was

We'll all go out

The same way

Told my younger self

Stay strong

Don't break

Told my younger self

Hold faith

Be great

Protect what you made

Don't wish for a rainy day

Fear/Fly

What's gonna keep me

Between life and pearly gates

Scares dug my grave

Let everything go

Never could fly

Lost my wings long ago

Trapped by parallels

Taught me too well

Neglect my wellness

Boatload of wealth

Never taught how to be a man

Only how to become the man

Against the hate

Supposed I'd soar

On this bed

Tucked between pillows

Softness replaced by hollowness

When I Thought It Was

Never the nectar

Only the encore pleased by pressure

Day by day

Floating below the pay raise

Night after night

Saw what enemies made

Chance after chance

Bottomed out

Saw how glass breaks

My ceiling couldn't wait

Still here

Tagged in by fear

What's holding me there

Lit the match

I'll fight back

Set the principle with me

The program wouldn't ease

Became what I feared

Antagonized to feel

Won't be a problem

Share the same day

Where is my plate

Nobody saw red

Like me

5th time I couldn't get up

This week

Crippled

Broken

Heartless wishing to find peace

Who gave me wings

When I found out

I'll probably cry

Note to myself

Don't have another choice

Except to try

See what they saw

I'll have my chance to fly

Blurry

Obliged happiness keeps us sold

Red as my soul

Never fitted for gameday

Moment in time

Never could glance

Seen forefathers put to rest

Should've had their wings

Our life

Made it better

Saw the other side

Eyes blurry

Hope this ain't heaven

Tattoos

Spread the word

Let me be

Tattoos

Saved my everything

Two months later

Thoughts of death kept me secure

Finally saw the light

When people ask

Show them why I fight

Since I'm older

I won't neglect

Bless it when I can

Cherish more than the fullest extent

Saw wins left in trash

Money was looking thin

On my eleven toes

Had to find my why

When I Thought It Was

Now and again

I feel tortured

Why build a bear

When it's all right here

Wish haters were right

And I was wrong

Revisioned my life

I'll be gone

What if

My people never fled

What if

My time wasn't there

Fell short of expectations

How I expect others to grow

Passages

Used to play with grass
Eternal soul from another past
Asked my dad if pain was real
Whoever took my smile....

Wish I knew the words
My tree grew with thorns
Memories fell from beneath
Reciting my past grief
This pen
Only bridge I'll see

Chapter 6

Tribute to Hazel

Crown

Took my final bow

God knew

Became prince when butter grew

Turned to vices

Treated my habits

Tell me

How much a dollar really cost

Guess none of us heard

Eternal strife and struggle

We're not onboard

Unhealed wounds

Room full of hurt

Price for my soul

Stood with the crowd

Sacrificed my life to Christ

Wasn't much of a fight

Don't handcuff them

I didn't suffice

When I Thought It Was

On this stand

Crown on my head

Took the charge

The man I should've become

Energy

Ripples from heaven

Crowned with a present

Grim days haunt me

 Deep in closure

Not feeling right

Sickness ripped my body clean

Fighting within

Above or beyond that soil

Behind the corner we'll see

Our own can't be

Aren't nurtured

Until there laid to rest

Sacrificed everything

Don't lend me anything

Used all of me

What people see

When it comes to me

When I Thought It Was

Never let greed outreach me

Our soul will outlive us

This soul will outlive me

Speak

Shattered our existence

Took my supreme being

Me and you

Everybody and us

Only ones to reap healing

Crashed and burned

Brothers and sisters

Lock hands and turn

Faced this reality

Why must I speak

Enemies boastful and conscious

Depleted souls multiple

What did the mortal man see

When they looked at me

Just another statistic

For the world

The white man

To see

If that's me

Then let me be

When I Thought It Was

Let me rest

You put them to sleep

Why ponder

If you ask

Why don't I speak

Ask yourself

Why can't I bleed

We're all human beings

Look and see

Find yourself

You and I know

We're not the same league

Y'all saw red

We felt blues

After years and years

Still won't speak

To what was true

And that's okay

Depiction

Carve out my drive

Reached in my pocket

For profit

Why bother

Destroy what we made

Depict us as fallen

Far from gone

High off drugs and assault

Determine myself

If I fit your life

And your lies

Live to be hated

Among distress

My life before painted

Respect my essence

The one up high

Took me from your sight

Saw my life

When I Thought It Was

Please don't run

Pressure underneath angels

Protect me from lust

Carrier of wills

Trust won't be undone

Strength

Fought for my will

Everything it took

My book is finished

Without a saving grace

Not every ending

Has a story

Not every hero

Has a send-off

Heal of darkness

Ray of success

In whatever circumstance

I want to matter

I want to feel

In whatever domain

In whatever lane

In whatever story

They seek to spin

My life is a sight to behold

When I Thought It Was

Hope they hold my spirit

Just as tight

Strength in numbers

Need people to fight

Colors

From who to choose
Candy stores restored
Red or blue
Don't blame us

Saw colors our people embodied
Couldn't pick and choose
Took a chance
Enemies painted my mind grey

If anything else
My soul is made from gold
Color of the asphalt
Will tell you different
Hope they know

Feel the heart these people had
In massive lands
Masters took our hand
We're forever lost

When I Thought It Was

Let who you are

Bleed from within

Be entranced

Capture what others saw

They hate

What they can't create

Patterns won't be left

Black and white

White and black

Erase me from history

My sun will rise

Self

When the dust settles

I'll weather away

But

You have to stay

Pain resides close

Scar on my heart closed

You were there

Front row and center

For the world to never see

Appreciate yourself

For being you

My being stood tall

Because of you

Living

They say
Live for tomorrow
Rather live today

What I get out
Is what I put in
An angel said
Anything can be made from faith

Special to me
Only myself
Made it to 21
Applaud who helped
Wrist doesn't bleed
Trauma never pleads
Whatever life brings
Take it on the chin
Or knee

Provide for the ones that can't
If I fall

Tribute to Hazel

Catch up to the bag

Even if it's worn

It'll be worth even more

In our kids' hands

Broke by this world

But this world

Will save me

Reminded to keep peace

Underneath the fortitude

We'll never sink

Our core

Made me stand

On my two feet

Human Nature

Neither black nor white

When you look my way

Aura is pure

Couldn't fake

Soldiers upon soldiers

Think their seen

We all saw

What they wanted to see

Looked as the leader

Piece of the canvas

I haven't forgotten

Human nature

Don't let your time seal

Summer

Summer can't wait

Paradise beyond it's plain

We found our way

Couldn't stay face

Would never end

Tonight we cut

Our loose ends

Worked the summer

Needed a profit

Was heaven

Before it became an option

Childhood

Felt so long

Felt too good

Touched the sky

Senses worked

Traverse through time

Times like this exist

Wish grandma could see me live

Will forever be on my hip

Life engraved in stone

Too soon

Went by so fast

Felt confirmed

Touched souls

Never will I love another

Like her

Went to her cemetery

Tears in my eyes

Now I know why

Tribute to Hazel

Swear on my oath

My people will see life

We'll be alright

Rip Mac Miller

It ain't 2009 no more

14 years later

Finally want more

Protect their heart

Means too much

Entering adulthood

With a faulty dream

Covered in smoke

But they'll see

Where it was life

Just life

Decipher when to get mad

Or cry

When greatness was a mirror away

Hazel saw it first

My life

When I Thought It Was

A tribute to her

Childhood

Held me close

Period that defined me

Long life ahead of me

Won't stop

Till grandma proud of me

Self Note

Please don't hurt yourself

Don't abuse

Understand your power

 Will change the world around you

Death eats at you whole

Heaven on earth

Carries so much mold

People will carve their blessings

 For you

Please note

You're in so many souls

Don't sacrifice yourself

 For the greater good

Don't have to be Robin Hood

 To receive love

Don't leave your future

If you stuck in the present

At the end of the tunnel

Be that someone to hug

When I Thought It Was

Lot of time left

Don't leave what you started

My message to you

You know you got this

Chapter 7

The Saving Grace

Freedom

Lay of the land

Price of my freedom

Offed with treason

Gave them every reason

Was worth it

For freedom

No weary eyes

If I die

This earth is mines

Soil engraved

Tell them my name

Everything you need

It's yours

Seal your heart

Heal yourself

Never be a hollow soul again

Destiny

Did I make it
Blame it on me

Faced the heavens
Above the rim
Fighting with toys
Before I fought the man
Win or lose
Gave it my all

For my future son
For my future daughter
Make a change
The world will be proud of

Played my cards
Held that flag
Destiny awaits
In the palm
Of loved one's hand

Stun Lock

Everyone on the couch

Counting 9 lives

My locked jaw survived

Time is surreal

Life is enough

Feening for spotlight

Cameras enforced law

Force-fed this world

Curtains closed

Won't see me swirl

Fighting the good fight

Couldn't open my eyes

Life let me by

Let my people down

Asked how high

He responded how far

24 hours till greatness

Still in pause

Body on the floor

Met with more

Concealed demons

Shared our reason

Brain hit autopilot

Swerving without fear

Meant more than

Being on that pill

Tripping in that field

That Time

Envisioned my tunnel

Created new life

Worthier than mines

They'll grow like a rose

If they take my dreams

Flourish behind

What was me

Went without peace

Revolution is coming

Behind that wall

Enough for me

Scared to cross

Couldn't be me

Capitalize off my struggle

My gift to you

That's the goal

That's my reason

Through thick and thin

The Saving Grace

We stand on hearts

Written in stars

Blessed

My people released at last

The End, For Now

Stay in the fight

We need you

This ain't the end

Even goodbye

We'll meet again

In the next life

Took my life for granted

Have to pay the price

Able to see light

Don't jeopardize your life

The love you've given

Said I'm the strongest

Truly believe different

Don't bleed different

In due time

They'll see why

Pen outta ink

Still going

The Saving Grace

It's your time

Don't forget

With you

We'll accomplish our reason

Survive

One step at a time

The end for now

Ima need time

In 5 years

We'll have what's ours

Love y'all more than myself

Broken Hearts Heal

Lead you to the life

You always wanted

We'll meet again

Look back

At what we started

Acknowledgements

Special thanks to:

Aaron	*Jevo*
Aunt Patrice	*Kanye West*
Black Matt	*Lucki*
Broken Hearts Heal	*Mom*
Chris	*Mr.File*
Dad	*Mr.Kiyoshi*
Dakota	*Mr.Sanchez*
Damari	*Mrs.Menjivar*
Denjoli	*Mrs.Treva*
Earl Sweatshirt	*Ms.Dey*
Frank Ocean	*Ms.Jess*
Galen	*Reyna*
Granny	*Tupac*
Steven	*Uncle Donny*
Isaiah	*Uncle Damane*
Isaiah C.	*Uncle Ked*
Isaiah H.	*Victoria*
Isaiah Rashad	*03 Greedo*
Javier	

The End

www.ingramcontent.com/pod-product-compliance
Lightning Source LLC
Chambersburg PA
CBHW070721130626
46553CB00005B/2087